CELEBRATING THE SPECIAL DAY
OF A **SPECIAL** PERSON.

PRESENTED TO

_____

FROM

_____

ON THIS DATE

_____

LITTLE
BIRTHDAY
SURPRISES

(WISHING YOU THE UNEXPECTED ON YOUR SPECIAL DAY)

REBECCA GERMANY

A DAYMAKER GREETING BOOK

ON YOUR BIRTHDAY MAY YOU...

FIND A FORGOTTEN **$20 BILL**

IN THE POCKET OF YOUR JEANS.

DISCOVER A FLOWER IN A SIDEWALK CRACK.

GAZE UPON A RAINBOW.

HAVE SOMEONE SPECIAL SMILE AT YOU.

RECEIVE A *handwritten* LETTER IN THE MAIL.

FIND SOMETHING **OLD** BUT *new*

TO WEAR IN YOUR CLOSET.

HAVE ALL YOUR FRIENDS REMEMBER
YOUR DAY AND <u>UNDERESTIMATE</u> YOUR AGE.

EAT CAKE FROM YOUR FAVORITE BAKERY.

ENJOY HAIR THAT STAYS IN *perfect* PLACE.

DETECT NEW WIGGLE ROOM

IN YOUR WAISTLINE.

BECOME THE WINNING,
ONE-MILLIONTH SHOPPER.

GET A kiss FROM YOUR SWEETHEART.

DISCOVER THERE'S STILL **ONE MORE**

ICE CREAM BAR IN THE FREEZER.

LEARN YOU UNDERESTIMATED THE AMOUNT
OF **MONEY** IN YOUR BANK ACCOUNT.

DETERMINE YOU CAN TEACH
AN OLD DOG A *new* TRICK.

HEAR YOUR FAVORITE SONG ON THE RADIO.

LOCATE A *free-meal* COUPON
FROM YOUR FAVORITE RESTAURANT.

EXPERIENCE **SOMETHING** THAT REMINDS YOU
THAT ANGELS ARE WATCHING OVER YOU.

BUMP INTO AN OLD FRIEND

YOU HAVEN'T SEEN IN A 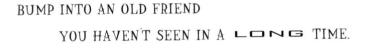 TIME.

FIND A LOST ROLL OF FILM YOU CAN DEVELOP
AND ENJOY RELIVING OLD MEMORIES.

DO SOMETHING THAT MAKES YOU
FEEL LIKE A kid AGAIN.

FIND AN EXTRA HOUR IN THE DAY SO THAT
YOU CAN REALLY *pamper* YOURSELF.

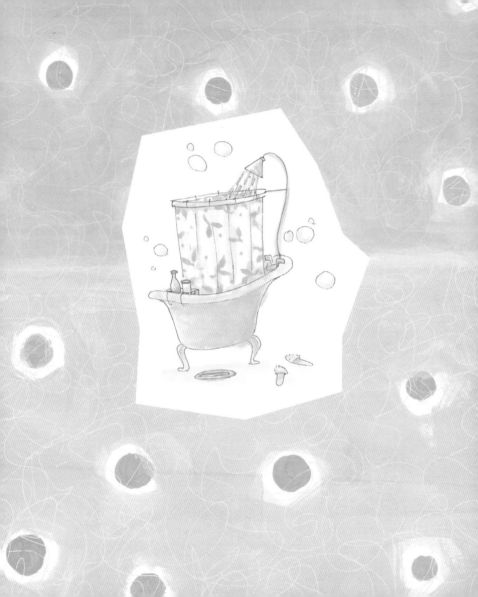

ANSWER THE PHONE AND HEAR

"I LOVE YOU."

DECIDE THE FACE IN THE MIRROR

LOOKS *pretty good* INDEED.

RECEIVE AN ANSWER TO PRAYER.

READ A SCRIPTURE **PROMISE** TO CARRY
WITH YOU THROUGH THE YEAR.

Delight yourself in the Lord
and he will give you
the desires of your heart.

PSALM 37:4 NIV

DayMaker
GREETING BOOKS

© 2004 by Barbour Publishing, Inc.

ISBN 1-59310-319-0

Designed by Greg Jackson, www.jacksondesignco.com.

Published by Barbour Publishing, Inc., P.O. Box 719, Uhrichsville, Ohio 44683, www.barbourbooks.com

*Our mission is to publish and distribute inspirational products
offering exceptional value and biblical encouragement to the masses.*

Member of the
Evangelical Christian
Publishers Association

Printed in China.
5 4 3 2 1